Boost Your Reading Skills

CEFR **A2**

BOOK 1

Success
with
Reading

Maiko Ikeda

Ayaka Shimizu

Michelle Witte

Zachary Fillingham

Gregory John Bahlmann

SEIBIDO

photographs

iStockphoto

音声ファイルのダウンロード／ストリーミング

CDマーク表示がある箇所は、音声を弊社HPより無料でダウンロード／ストリーミングすることができます。トップページのバナーをクリックし、書籍検索してください。書籍詳細ページに音声ダウンロードアイコンがございますのでそちらから自習用音声としてご活用ください。

https://www.seibido.co.jp

 ### ActeaBo

本書はテキスト連動型Web教材ActeaBoに対応しています。ActeaBoでは、各Unitに2編ずつ新たな英文素材が用意されており、授業で学んだリーディング方略や内容理解問題で振り返り学習することができます（本書をご利用期間中の1年間）。ActeaBoのご利用については、先生の指示に従い、ID、パスワードを取得後、下記URLよりアクセスしてください。

http://acteabo.jp

ID	
パスワード	

※本サービスは教育機関におけるクラス単位でのご利用に限らせていただきます。

Preface

Success with Reading Book 1 —Boost Your Reading Skills— is the first book of a three-volume series designed mainly to develop reading skills with the aid of learning strategies. High proficiency in English will broaden your horizons and enable you to see a more interesting world.

Each unit of *Success with Reading Book 1* follows a set structure to encourage students to put what they have learned into practice in communication activities. The unit begins with a Tips for Reading section, which introduces a strategy for more effective reading. This is followed by a Vocabulary section in which students check words related to the topic in context. They will then check their comprehension of the passage, both details and main ideas. The unit ends with opportunities for students to express and exchange their ideas regarding the related topics.

As students progress through each level, they are constantly encouraged to put what they have learned to use. At the same time, they never stop taking new challenges that will push them to a new stage. *Success with Reading Book 1* will open up a path to a place where students can look out over a wonderful landscape after enjoying every moment of the journey.

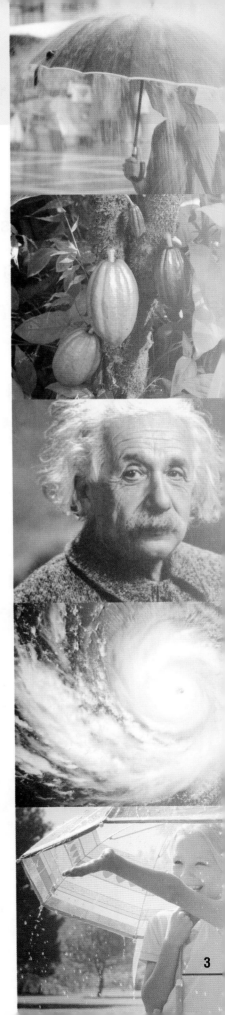

Contents

KEY FOR LEARNING 1
Remembering new words with sounds

KEY FOR LEARNING 2
Remembering new words in context

KEY FOR LEARNING 3
Learning vocabulary with prefixes and suffixes

Learning Overview

KEY FOR LEARNING 1

UNIT 1 Remembering new words with sounds

Amazing Chocolates

WARM-UP QUESTIONS

Discuss the questions below with your classmates.

1. How often do you eat chocolate in a week?
2. When do you think was chocolate first sold in Japan?

VOCABULARY 🎧 2

From the choices below, choose the word which fits best in each sentence.

1. In the English alphabet, the letter M _____ the letter L.
2. Would you like to _____ sugar to your coffee?
3. There are many different _____ in the world, such as Buddhism and Islam.
4. My father could not _____ to buy such an expensive toy for me.
5. We regularly clean the playground to _____ our community.
6. Herbal tea has healing _____.
7. We need to put the same _____ of sugar and flour into the bowl.
8. They all laughed, with the _____ of Taro.
9. This webpage _____ a lot of useful information for tourists in Japan.
10. The heavy rain _____ my new shoes.

add	afford	amount	benefit	contains
exception	follows	properties	religions	ruined

10

---

1 — WARM-UP QUESTIONS

Introduces warm-up questions to activate the students' background knowledge about the topic.

2 — VOCABULARY

Teaches topic-related vocabulary words in a sentence where students can learn the usage of the words.

TIPS FOR READING

Remembering new words with sounds (1)

A first step to successful reading is increasing your vocabulary. Remembering a new word by using sounds works very well for your brain. When you see a word for the first time, you link it to its meaning through its sounds (seeing → sounds → meaning). After your brain takes this route many times, it skips sounds to reach the meaning. In order to build a shortcut, you can start learning vocabulary by checking its pronunciation.

It may be helpful to use an electronic or on-line dictionary. Below are some examples of useful online dictionaries. Which one is your favorite?

Example

Cambridge Dictionary
Has both English-Japanese and English-English dictionaries.
https://dictionary.cambridge.org/ja/

Longman Dictionary of Contemporary English Online
Useful for beginners using a monolingual dictionary. Has many useful example sentences.
https://www.ldoceonline.com/

Merriam-Webster Unabridged Dictionary
Useful for checking words with similar meanings (= thesaurus).
https://www.merriam-webster.com/

EXERCISE

Check the pronunciation of the words in the Vocabulary Section.
If you are not sure about the pronunciation, check it with a dictionary.

Words to Check

11

3 — TIPS FOR READING

Teaches a reading strategy together with examples and key points.

EXERCISE

Provides an opportunity for using tips for reading introduced above.

4 READING PASSAGE

Features an interesting article from a variety of topics. Also, it provides an other opportunity for using tips for reading introduced in the unit.

READING PASSAGE 🔊 3

Read the passage below and focus on the sound of the words.

◦ Chocolate

Do you like chocolate? Most people love it. Its sweet, creamy flavor is hard to resist. But where did chocolate come from?

About 2,600 years ago, the Olmec, who lived in Central and South America made use of chocolate. They used cocoa beans to make a special drink, but this drink was not sweet like the chocolate we are used to. It was very bitter. In the years that followed, they started adding other things to their cocoa drink to make it taste better.

Chocolate was very important for the Maya, another group in Central America. Mayans used cocoa beans as money, and it is said that 10 beans could buy a rabbit. Cocoa beans were also used in Mayan religion and wedding ceremonies. The Mayans also used cocoa beans to make a chocolate drink, but only rich people could afford to drink it.

When the Europeans arrived in South America, they started to bring this popular drink back to their home countries. Milk, cream, and sugar were added, and eventually the chocolate we know was born. In the year 1689, chocolate milk was developed in Jamaica.

Chocolate is now one of the most popular flavors in the world. In modern society, we can enjoy chocolate in bars, ice cream, cakes, milkshakes, pies, and many other foods. Some studies have found that dark chocolate is good for our health because it benefits the circulatory

◦ Chocolate is created from cocoa beans.

system and has other anticancer properties. Thus, small but regular amounts of dark chocolate might be able to reduce the risk of a heart attack.

Nothing is perfect, and chocolate is no exception. Chocolate can contain a large amount of calories, so people who eat a lot of chocolate risk becoming obese. Perhaps the secret to enjoying chocolate's flavor and not ruining your health is very simple: do not eat too much of it!

◦ Mayan writing referring to cocoa (Wikipedia)

◦ A Mayan chief forbids a person to touch a jar of chocolate. (cc by Mayan Civilization)

COMPREHENSION QUESTIONS

Decide if each statement is true [T] or false [F]. If it is false, correct it.

1. [ ] The Maya changed the chocolate drink to make its taste better.
2. [ ] In Mayan society, one rabbit cost 10 beans.
3. [ ] The familiar taste of chocolate existed before Europeans arrived in South America.
4. [ ] Eating chocolate regularly may cause a heart attack.
5. [ ] Eating a large amount of chocolate causes obesity.

12   13

---

6 GRAPHIC SUMMARY

Introduces a summary-writing exercise which is also useful as an output activity.

GRAPHIC SUMMARY

Complete the outline notes below. You can look at the passage if you want.

AMAZING CHOCOLATES

1 History of chocolate

About 2,600 years ago in Central and South America

- The Olmec used cocoa beans to make a special drink.
- At first, it was sweet but very 1. _____.
- The Maya used cocoa beans as 2. _____.
- They also used beans for 3. _____, wedding ceremonies, and a drink.
  - Only rich people could 4. _____ it.

When Europeans arrived in South America

- They brought the chocolate drink 5. _____ to Europe.
- They 6. _____ milk, cream, and sugar.

In 1689 in Jamaica

- Chocolate milk was 7. _____.

2 For Health

- Dark chocolate 8. _____ the circulatory system and has other anticancer 9. _____.
- Eating too much chocolate could 10. _____ your health.

14

---

5 COMPREHENSION QUESTIONS

Introduces comprehension exercises based on the content from Reading passage.

7 WRITING AND DISCUSSION

Introduces questions for output exercise based on the content of the reading passage.

WRITING AND DISCUSSION

Read the questions below and write down your ideas or opinions. Exchange your ideas or opinions with your classmates. Use the hints if you want.

1. What do you eat or drink regularly to keep yourself healthy?

   Hints ☺ well-balanced meals / protein drinks / green tea

   Your Ideas
   _____
   _____
   _____
   _____

2. What is your favorite food? How is it eaten in other towns or countries?

   Hints ☺ bananas / fried food / *niku-jaga* / pork instead of beef

   Your Ideas
   _____
   _____
   _____
   _____

FURTHER STUDY

For further study, access ActeaBo and review today's lesson.

http://acteabo.jp

15

8 FURTHER STUDY

Introduces an opportunity for further independent study.

For successful English learning, one of the most important things is to CONTINUE learning it. You cannot master English by studying only for a couple of years. English learning is therefore very similar to climbing mountains, practicing cooking or practicing a music instrument. You need to continue.

However, you cannot continue to learn English without a CLEAR GOAL to achieve. For example, when it comes to climbing a mountain, how high is the mountain? What tools or clothes do you need for climbing? Which route are you going to take? How many days do you need? Without knowing all of this clearly, you cannot maintain your motivation and may soon give up.

Therefore, you need to set a clear goal before restarting your English learning this time. The clearer it is, the more easily you can achieve it. Also, setting SMALLER STEPS to achieve the goal helps you continue learning. Every time you take one step forward, you can feel success and the desire to move forward.

Example

Goal	Reading one passage easily without using a dictionary
Smaller steps	1. Increasing vocabulary (300 more words) 2. Reading faster ← arriving here one year later! 3. Writing a short summary (with a few sentences)

LET'S TRY

Set a clear goal for your English learning. Also, set smaller steps to achieve the goal. Do not forget to indicate where you want to be one year later through learning English with this textbook.

Goal	
Smaller steps	

Amazing Chocolates

WARM-UP QUESTIONS

Discuss the questions below with your classmates.

1. How often do you eat chocolate in a week?
2. When do you think was chocolate first sold in Japan?

VOCABULARY 🖸 2

From the choices below, choose the word which fits best in each sentence.

1. In the English alphabet, the letter M _____ the letter L.
2. Would you like to _____ sugar to your coffee?
3. There are many different _____ in the world, such as Buddhism and Islam.
4. My father could not _____ to buy such an expensive toy for me.
5. We regularly clean the playground to _____ our community.
6. Herbal tea has healing _____.
7. We need to put the same _____ of sugar and flour into the bowl.
8. They all laughed, with the _____ of Taro.
9. This webpage _____ a lot of useful information for tourists in Japan.
10. The heavy rain _____ my new shoes.

add	afford	amount	benefit	contains
exception	follows	properties	religions	ruined

Remembering new words with sounds (1)

A first step to successful reading is increasing your vocabulary. Remembering a new word by using sounds works very well for your brain. When you see a word for the first time, you link it to its meaning through its sounds (seeing → sounds → meaning). After your brain takes this route many times, it skips sounds to reach the meaning. In order to build a shortcut, you can start learning vocabulary by checking its pronunciation.

It may be helpful to use an electronic or on-line dictionary. Below are some examples of useful online dictionaries. Which one is your favorite?

Example

Cambridge Dictionary
Has both English-Japanese and English-English dictionaries.
https://dictionary.cambridge.org/ja/

Longman Dictionary of Contemporary English Online
Useful for beginners using a monolingual dictionary.
Has many useful example sentences.
https://www.ldoceonline.com/

Merriam-Webster Unabridged Dictionary
Useful for checking words with similar meanings (= thesaurus).
https://www.merriam-webster.com/

EXERCISE
Check the pronunciation of the words in the Vocabulary Section.
If you are not sure about the pronunciation, check it with a dictionary.

> **Words to Check**

UNIT 1 AMAZING CHOCOLATES
UNIT 2
UNIT 3
UNIT 4
UNIT 5
UNIT 6
UNIT 7
UNIT 8
UNIT 9
UNIT 10
UNIT 11
UNIT 12
UNIT 13
UNIT 14

READING PASSAGE 3

Read the passage below and focus on the sound of the words.

>> Chocolate

1   Do you like chocolate? Most people love it. Its sweet, creamy flavor is hard to resist. But where did chocolate come from?

2   About 2,600 years ago, the Olmec, who lived in Central and South America made use of chocolate. They used cocoa beans to make a special drink, but this drink was not sweet like the chocolate we are used to. It was very bitter. In the years that followed, they started adding other things to their cocoa drink to make it taste better.

3 Chocolate was very important for the Maya, another group in Central America. Mayans used cocoa beans as money, and it is said that 10 beans could buy a rabbit. Cocoa beans were also used in Mayan religion and wedding ceremonies. The Mayans also used cocoa beans to make a chocolate drink, but only rich people could afford to drink it.

4 When the Europeans arrived in South America, they started to bring this popular drink back to their home countries. Milk, cream, and sugar were added, and eventually the chocolate we know was born. In the year 1689, chocolate milk was developed in Jamaica.

5 Chocolate is now one of the most popular flavors in the world. In modern society, we can enjoy chocolate in bars, ice cream, cakes, milkshakes, pies, and many other foods. Some studies have found that dark chocolate is good for our health because it benefits the circulatory

⌃ Chocolate is created from cocoa beans.

UNIT 1

AMAZING CHOCOLATES

UNIT 2
UNIT 3
UNIT 4
UNIT 5
UNIT 6
UNIT 7
UNIT 8
UNIT 9
UNIT 10
UNIT 11
UNIT 12
UNIT 13
UNIT 14

30 system and has other anticancer properties. Thus, small but regular amounts of dark chocolate might be able to reduce the risk of a heart attack.

6 Nothing is perfect, and chocolate is no exception. Chocolate can contain a large amount of calories, so people who eat a lot of chocolate risk becoming obese. Perhaps the secret to enjoying chocolate's flavor and not ruining your health is very simple: do not eat too much of it!

⌃ Mayan writing referring to cocoa
(Wikipedia)

⌃ A Mayan chief forbids a person to touch a jar of chocolate.
(cc by Mayan Civilisation)

COMPREHENSION QUESTIONS

Decide if each statement is true [T] or false [F]. If it is false, correct it.

1. [   ] The Maya changed the chocolate drink to make its taste better.
2. [   ] In Mayan society, one rabbit cost 10 beans.
3. [   ] The familiar taste of chocolate existed before Europeans arrived in South America.
4. [   ] Eating chocolate regularly may cause a heart attack.
5. [   ] Eating a large amount of chocolate causes obesity.

Complete the outline notes below. You can look at the passage if you want.

AMAZING CHOCOLATES

1 History of chocolate

About 2,600 years ago in Central and South America

- The Olmec used cocoa beans to make a special drink.
- At first, it was not sweet but very 1. _____ .
- The Maya used cocoa beans as 2. _____ .
- They also used beans for 3. _____ and wedding ceremonies, and a drink.

Only rich people could 4. _____ it.

When Europeans arrived in South America

- They brought the chocolate drink 5. _____ to Europe.
- They 6. _____ milk, cream, and sugar.

In 1689 in Jamaica

- Chocolate milk was 7. _____ .

2 For Health

- Dark chocolate 8. _____ the circulatory system and has other anticancer 9. _____ .
- Eating too much chocolate could 10. _____ your health.

UNIT 1

AMAZING CHOCOLATES

UNIT 2
UNIT 3
UNIT 4
UNIT 5
UNIT 6
UNIT 7
UNIT 8
UNIT 9
UNIT 10
UNIT 11
UNIT 12
UNIT 13
UNIT 14

WRITING AND DISCUSSION

Read the questions below and write down your ideas or opinions. Exchange your ideas or opinions with your classmates. Use the hints if you want.

1. What do you eat or drink regularly to keep yourself healthy?

   Hints ➡ well-balanced meals / protein drinks / green tea

   > **Your Ideas**
   > ....
   > ....
   > ....
   > ....
   > ....

2. What is your favorite food? How is it eaten in other towns or countries?

   Hints ➡ bananas / fried food / *niku-jaga* / pork instead of beef

   > **Your Ideas**
   > ....
   > ....
   > ....
   > ....
   > ....

FURTHER STUDY

For further study, access ActeaBo and review today's lesson.

http://acteabo.jp

UNIT 2

Jokes

WARM-UP QUESTIONS

Discuss the questions below with your classmates.

1. When was the last time you heard a joke?
2. In what situations do people tell jokes?

VOCABULARY 🔘 4

From the choices below, choose the word which fits best in each sentence.

1. The town _____ heavily on tourism.
2. The film kept us in _____ until the very end.
3. Hard work is an important _____ of his success.
4. By the next meeting, please _____ this document from Japanese into English.
5. To understand what these messages mean, we must put them in _____.
6. The _____ is that the richest countries have the least natural resources.
7. I find his behavior towards you very _____.
8. The cafeteria is only open at _____ times of day.
9. People walked for _____ equality together with Martin Luther King Jr.
10. Even the _____ experts could not explain what happened.

certain	context	depends	element	insulting
irony	racial	supposed	suspense	translate

Remembering new words with sounds (2)

Using sounds to remember new words does not always mean listening to the sounds. Reading the words aloud is also an easy and effective way. By reading them aloud, you can pay more attention to their sounds.

EXERCISE

Make pairs (Students A and B).

Student A: Read each sentence aloud in the Vocabulary Section for Student B.
Do not show your textbook to Student B.

Student B: Close your textbook, and repeat after Student A.
If you get stuck, ask Student A for a hint.

READING PASSAGE 5

Read the passage below listening to the sounds of the words.

1   Jokes are things we say to make other people laugh. Sometimes a joke is a short remark, while other times it can be a story that can take some time to tell. There are lots of ways that jokes make people laugh.

2   Here are examples of two simple jokes:

Why do birds fly south?

Because it's too far to walk.

Why do hummingbirds hum?

Because they don't know the words.

5 **3**   Most people like to laugh, and people who tell jokes well are often popular. But there is more to a joke than just the words; a joke depends on the way it is told. Jokes depend on building suspense. The humor in many jokes 10 also depends on using the element of surprise, so the joke teller has to be a good actor. Some people have a knack for telling jokes; others do not.

UNIT 1

JOKES

UNIT 2

UNIT 3

UNIT 4

UNIT 5

UNIT 6

UNIT 7

UNIT 8

UNIT 9

UNIT 10

UNIT 11

UNIT 12

UNIT 13

UNIT 14

4   Not all jokes can be saved by the way they are told, however. We say a
15 joke is "corny" if it is not funny or if it is stupid. This is a corny joke:

Why did the chicken cross the road?

To get to the other side.

Of course, some people, like me, really like corny jokes!

5   Every language and culture has its own jokes, and many jokes lose their
humor when translated into a different language or cultural context. Some
jokes rely on sarcasm or irony to be funny. However, these jokes can be rude or
20 insulting.

6   Sometimes jokes are told about certain races and religions. These are
called "racial" and "religious" jokes, and they can be insulting, too. Jokes
about the supposed special characteristics of a gender are often called "sexist."
Hurting people's feelings really should not be funny. There are plenty of other
25 ways to make people laugh. Have you heard a good joke lately?

COMPREHENSION QUESTIONS

Decide if each statement is true [T] *or false* [F]. *If it is false, correct
it.*

1. [   ] Jokes can take two forms: a short remark or a story.

2. [   ] People who often tell jokes are usually popular.

3. [   ] Everyone has a talent for telling jokes.

4. [   ] We should avoid religious jokes.

5. [   ] Sexist jokes are about a specific gender's characteristics that
   some people mistakenly believe to be true.

Complete the outline notes below. You can look at the passage if you want.

JOKES

1 Jokes are ...

- things we say to make other people 1. [____]

2 Good jokes depend on ...

- the way they are told
- building 2. [____]
- using the element of 3. [____]

  * Jokes may 4. [____] their humor if you translate them
  into a different 5. [____] .

3 Bad jokes include ...

- 6. [____] or irony
- 7. [____] and religious jokes
- supposed special characteristics of a 8. [____] (= sexist)

- 9. [____] jokes are bad.
- We do not use jokes to 10. [____] people's feelings.

WRITING AND DISCUSSION

Read the questions below and write down your ideas or opinions. Exchange your ideas or opinions with your classmates. Use the hints if you want.

1. Do you see any cultural differences in the frequency or way of telling jokes? Why?

   Hints ➲ Kansai area / business / relationships

   > **Your Ideas**
   >
   > ....
   >
   > ....
   >
   > ....
   >
   > ....

2. What are the advantages of making people laugh?

   Hints ➲ breaking the ice / health / feel relaxed

   > **Your Ideas**
   >
   > ....
   >
   > ....
   >
   > ....
   >
   > ....

FURTHER STUDY

For further study, access ActeaBo and review today's lesson.

http://acteabo.jp

The First Money

WARM-UP QUESTIONS

Discuss the questions below with your classmates.

1. What are banknotes and coins made of in Japan? How about those in other countries?

2. What kind of things did people use as money in the past?

VOCABULARY   6

From the choices below, choose the word which fits best in each sentence.

1. A group of _____ started a new project on AI.

2. You can change the colors of the cloth by mixing a food _____ into water.

3. When he landed on the shore, he found the _____ people of America.

4. We have similar _____ in foods; both of us like spicy foods.

5. You should not _____ anything in the room when you go out.

6. He traveled into town to _____ the vegetables from this farm.

7. After the party, we _____ email addresses to keep in contact with each other.

8. The box looks heavy, but it _____ only a few kilograms.

9. I will call you back later. Is two o'clock _____ for you?

10. Your new passport will be _____ within a month.

aboriginal	convenient	dye	exchanged	issued
leave	scientists	taste	trade	weighs

Remembering new words in context (1)

You can remember a new word (e.g., glad) better if you memorize it in a sample sentence. Remembering a sentence is more difficult than remembering a word. However, a sentence gives a context or story for the word. The sentence can become a hint to help you remember the word.

Making your own sample sentences will help you even more, because things related to you tend to stay longer in your memory.

Example

glad → I am glad to have you as a guest.

EXERCISE

From the Vocabulary Section, choose words you do not know. For each of them, make your own sample sentences. Then, compare your sentences with your classmates. You can also make use of example sentences in dictionaries.

Word to remember	Your own sample sentence

UNIT 1
UNIT 2
UNIT 3
THE FIRST MONEY
UNIT 4
UNIT 5
UNIT 6
UNIT 7
UNIT 8
UNIT 9
UNIT 10
UNIT 11
UNIT 12
UNIT 13
UNIT 14

>> Stone money on the island of Yap

READING PASSAGE  7

Read the passage below and pay attention to new words.

1 Everyone loves money, but do you know where money originally came from? Do you know who were the first people to use money? Scientists say that over 10,000 years ago, people in Swaziland, Southern Africa, were using red dye as a type of money. The aboriginal people

5 of Australia were also using a similar dye as a type of money around that period of time. Later, people in several other parts of the world used shells and other valuable things to buy or trade for things they wanted. This is known as a barter system, a form of trade where some goods are exchanged for other goods.

10 **2** Many things have been used as money, from pigs to spices to salt. For a long time, pepper could be used to pay for things in Europe. On the Micronesian island of Yap, people used very big stone "coins," some of which were up to eight feet wide and weighed more than a small car.

3 However, the most convenient forms of money were pieces of valuable

15 metals like gold and silver. Historians think that the Lydians were the first

The first coins were made by the Lydians out of an alloy of gold and silver. (cc by Classical Numismatic Group, Inc. http://www. cngcoins.com)

people to introduce the use of gold and silver coins around 650 BC. Gold and silver are still quite valuable today.

UNIT 1
UNIT 2
UNIT 3
THE FIRST MONEY
UNIT 4
UNIT 5
UNIT 6
UNIT 7
UNIT 8
UNIT 9
UNIT 10
UNIT 11
UNIT 12
UNIT 13
UNIT 14

4 The first banknotes appeared in
20 China in the seventh century, and the
first banknotes in Europe were issued in
1661.

5 Money has changed through the
ages, but it has always been important.
25 Whether it is paper or pigs, most people
like to have some money.

>> Song Dynasty jiaozi,
the world's earliest
paper money

COMPREHENSION QUESTIONS

Decide if each statement is true [T] or false [F]. If it is false, correct it.

1. [   ] People on different continents used dye as a type of money.
2. [   ] People in the past exchanged pigs for spices.
3. [   ] Coins used on the Micronesian island of Yap were very big.
4. [   ] Valuable metals began to be used in a barter system.
5. [   ] Banknotes appeared earlier in Europe than in China.

GRAPHIC SUMMARY

Complete the outline notes below. You can look at the passage if you want.

THE FIRST MONEY

1 Various types of money

- red **1.** _____ over 10,000 years ago
  in Swaziland (Southern Africa)
  also in **2.** _____

- shells

- pigs

- **3.** _____

- salt

- pepper (in Europe)

- big stones (on the Micronesian island of Yap)

  = eight feet **4.** _____ and **5.** _____ more than
  a small car

  ✳ used for barter system to **6.** _____ goods for other ones

2 Convenient forms of money

- **7.** _____ metals (e.g., gold and silver)

- first gold and silver **8.** _____ around 650 BC by Lydians

3 Banknotes

- first appeared in **9.** _____ in the 7th century

- first **10.** _____ in Europe in 1661

WRITING AND DISCUSSION

Read the questions below and write down your ideas or opinions. Exchange your ideas or opinions with your classmates. Use the hints if you want.

1. What did you buy when you first used money as a child?

   Hints ➲ sweets / gifts / comic books / shoes

   > **Your Ideas**
   >
   > ....
   > ....
   > ....
   > ....

2. Imagine something you would like to have now. You can get it only by using a barter system. Try to negotiate with your partner. What do you need to exchange for it? Report the result of your negotiation to the class.

   Hints ➲ a bowl of noodles / new glasses / meal preparation service

   > **Your Ideas**
   >
   > ....
   > ....
   > ....
   > ....

FURTHER STUDY

For further study, access ActeaBo and review today's lesson.

http://acteabo.jp

UNIT 1
UNIT 2
UNIT 3
THE FIRST MONEY
UNIT 4
UNIT 5
UNIT 6
UNIT 7
UNIT 8
UNIT 9
UNIT 10
UNIT 11
UNIT 12
UNIT 13
UNIT 14

White Noise

WARM-UP QUESTIONS

Discuss the questions below with your classmates.

1. What environment do you prefer when you study? Your room, a café, or a library? Why?

2. What environment helps you sleep well?

VOCABULARY 🖸 8

From the choices below, choose the word which fits best in each sentence.

1. You can check the _____ of a word in dictionaries.

2. In aromatherapy, different oils from plants are used in _____.

3. North is the _____ direction of south.

4. She turned on a radio to _____ the noise from outside.

5. Learning English is difficult because it is _____ from Japanese.

6. It is _____ when you are in a hurry and the traffic light does not change smoothly.

7. Each _____ employee received a bonus for Christmas.

8. It will _____ take about a few days for the package to arrive.

9. They could not _____ the patients because of a lack of medicine.

10. We may face a big _____ in our food supply in the near future.

annoying	combination	deficit	definition	distinct
individual	mask	opposite	probably	treat

Remembering new words in context (2)

Learning new words in context helps you remember them better. Also, it helps you understand how to use them.

Example   ✕ Yesterday was a <u>glad</u> day.
           ○ I am <u>glad</u> to see you today.

To pay attention to the usage, an output (=speaking or writing) activity is useful.

▎ EXERCISE

Translate the sample sentences in the Vocabulary Section into Japanese. Then, translate them back into English without looking at the original sentences.

1	Japanese	
	Back to English	
2	Japanese	
	Back to English	
3	Japanese	
	Back to English	
4	Japanese	
	Back to English	
5	Japanese	
	Back to English	
6	Japanese	
	Back to English	
7	Japanese	
	Back to English	
8	Japanese	
	Back to English	
9	Japanese	
	Back to English	
10	Japanese	
	Back to English	

UNIT 1
UNIT 2
UNIT 3
WHITE NOISE
UNIT 4
UNIT 5
UNIT 6
UNIT 7
UNIT 8
UNIT 9
UNIT 10
UNIT 11
UNIT 12
UNIT 13
UNIT 14

READING PASSAGE 9

Read the passage below and translate it into Japanese. Then, translate it back into English without looking at the original.

1   Have you ever noticed how, on a rainy night, all other sounds seem to disappear? The sound of the rain drowns them out. And even though the sound of the rain goes on all night, it does not keep you awake. Rain is a kind of white noise—a steady, unchanging, unobtrusive sound.

5 **2**   White noise is made up of sounds from all the frequencies a human ear can hear, with the sound at each frequency having equal power. It is called "white" because the definition is like that of white light, which is a combination of all the light wavelengths we can see. You might think that a combination of all possible sound frequencies

10 would be terrible, but it is not—quite the opposite. The reason for this is that white noise masks other sounds. Think of it like the rain: the sound of one drop falling, like from a leaky tap, would be very distinct and annoying. Two drops would be the same. You could even tell three steady drips apart. But if there were five or

⌃ **White noise has proved to be useful in alleviating migraines for some people.**

⌃ "White noise" image

≫ Rain is a kind of white noise.

30

UNIT 1

UNIT 2

UNIT 3

WHITE NOISE

UNIT 4

UNIT 5

UNIT 6

UNIT 7

UNIT 8

UNIT 9

UNIT 10

UNIT 11

UNIT 12

UNIT 13

UNIT 14

15 10 or 1,000, you could not pick out each individual drip. They would all blend into a sort of hum or a quiet roar and probably lull you to sleep.

3 The calming properties of white noise are starting to be used to treat different problems. White noise can help restless people sleep and help migraine sufferers sleep through their pain. It can be very useful for people 20 with attention deficit disorders, who have trouble tuning out background noise. White noise can help them concentrate. It is even used to mask the sound of individual conversations by therapists and others who want to maintain privacy. Who would have thought that mashing lots of sounds together would actually turn out to promote peace and quiet?

White Gaussian noise signal
(cc by Morn)

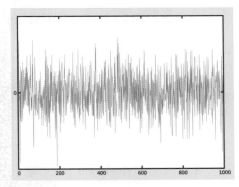

COMPREHENSION QUESTIONS

Decide if each statement is true [T] or false [F]. If it is false, correct it.

1. [   ] The sound of rain is an example of white noise.

2. [   ] Heavy rain at night frequently wakes you up.

3. [   ] White noise is a combination of sounds at different frequencies.

4. [   ] We do not notice the sound of a drop of water from the tap.

5. [   ] Scientists are trying to make use of white noise for many patients.

Complete the outline notes below. You can look at the passage if you want.

WHITE NOISE

1 **White noise is ...**

- a steady, 1. _____, unobtrusive sound
- made up of sounds from all the 2. _____ a human ear can hear

2 **Its characteristics**

- not 3. _____ and annoying

  ← 4. _____ other sounds

  e.g.) rain drops: they all 5. _____ into a sort of hum

3 **Different uses**

a) helping people concentrate

- for 6. _____ people to sleep
- for migraine 7. _____ to sleep through their pain
- for people with attention 8. _____ disorders

b) protecting 9. _____

- by 10. _____ conversations by therapists and patients

UNIT 1
UNIT 2
UNIT 3
UNIT 4
WHITE NOISE
UNIT 5
UNIT 6
UNIT 7
UNIT 8
UNIT 9
UNIT 10
UNIT 11
UNIT 12
UNIT 13
UNIT 14

WRITING AND DISCUSSION

Read the questions below and write down your ideas or opinions.
Exchange your ideas or opinions with your classmates. Use the hints
if you want.

1. What kind of sounds can or cannot be white noise?

Hints ➡ birds singing / people talking / classical music

Your Ideas

....
....
....
....

2. What else can white noise be used for?

Hints ➡ separate / classroom / baby's crying

Your Ideas

....
....
....
....

FURTHER STUDY

ActeaBo

For further study, access ActeaBo and review today's lesson.

http://acteabo.jp

UNIT 5

The Genius of Albert Einstein

WARM-UP QUESTIONS

Discuss the questions below with your classmates.

1. What do you know about Albert Einstein?
2. What kinds of Nobel Prize are there?

VOCABULARY CD 10

From the choices below, choose the word which fits best in each sentence.

1. There is no magic _____ for mastering another language without any effort.

2. Your seat belt should _____ fastened at all times.

3. We must _____ a means of transportation that does not cause sound pollution.

4. Using a computer to perform this type of _____ saves several hours.

5. After a long discussion, they _____ came up with a wonderful idea.

6. I have at last _____ the true secret to quitting sweets.

7. She _____ that it had been a difficult film to make.

8. My father is a retired _____ of educational studies.

9. Taro's name has become _____ with political scandal.

10. My father is an announcer, so he is a _____ at storytelling.

calculation	discovered	devise	eventually	explained
formula	genius	professor	remain	synonymous

Learning vocabulary with prefixes and suffixes (1)

English contains many words with prefixes (e.g. com-) and suffixes (e.g. -tion) because English imported many words from Greek and Latin-based languages. Each prefix and suffix has its own meaning, and so understanding them will help you increase your vocabulary.

Example

prefixes:	*dis*- (not)	*pro*- (forward, for)	*syn*- (same)
e.g.	dissatisfied disadvantage	propose produce	synchronize synthesize

suffixes:	*-ion* (making nouns)	*-ous* (making adjectives)	*-ate* (making verbs)
e.g.	preparation discussion	famous dangerous	decorate regulate

EXERCISE

With the prefixes and suffixes listed above, check the meaning of the words in the Vocabulary Section.

words	prefixes/ suffixes	meaning
calculation	cal- -ion	small stone making noun
discover		
device		
eventually		
explain		
formula		
genius		
professor		
remain		
synonymous		

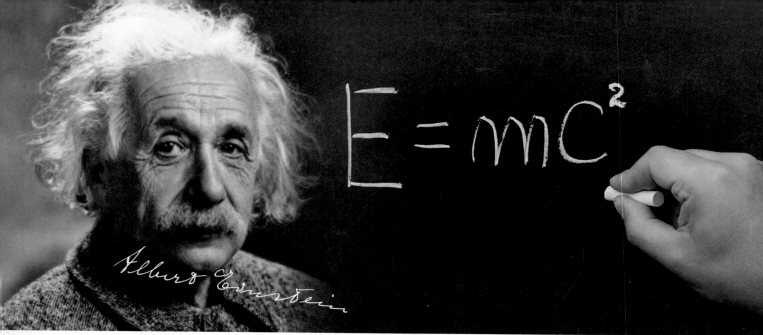

Einstein in 1947

READING PASSAGE 11

Read the passage below and check the meanings of new vocabulary with prefixes and suffixes.

1　You must have heard of the formula $E = mc^2$. This is still the most famous scientific formula ever worked out. It remains an important cornerstone of science, and devising it made the scientist Albert Einstein famous.

2　Before he published the calculations in 1905 that showed why $E = mc^2$,
5　scientists around the world strongly believed that $E = \frac{1}{2} mc^2$. Today, a high school physics student can do the calculations and understand what Albert Einstein did to become famous.

3　Albert Einstein was born into a Jewish family in Germany on March 14, 1879. He started to speak when he was three years old. Young Einstein did not
10　do well at school because he did not work hard in the classes that bored him. As a result, many people thought that he was stupid. Eventually he became interested in science and tried to discover a law of physics that would explain how everything in science works.

4　In 1922, he received the 1921 Nobel Prize in Physics. Later, he moved to
15　the United States and became a professor at Princeton University. In 1939, Einstein, together with Leo Szilard, a Hungarian-American physicist, wrote a letter to the US president, Franklin D. Roosevelt, saying that America should develop an atomic bomb before the Germans did. This letter resulted in the

UNIT 1
UNIT 2
UNIT 3
UNIT 4

THE GENIUS OF ALBERT EINSTEIN

UNIT 5
UNIT 6
UNIT 7
UNIT 8
UNIT 9
UNIT 10
UNIT 11
UNIT 12
UNIT 13
UNIT 14

⌃ Einstein received the 1921 Nobel Prize in Physics.

⌃ Einstein started to speak when he was three years old. (1882)

⌃ Einstein in 1935 at Princeton

development of the atomic bombs that would be dropped on the Japanese
20 cities of Hiroshima and Nagasaki in August 1945.

5 Einstein died in Princeton, New Jersey, on April 18, 1955. In his life,
more than 300 scientific works and over 150 nonscientific works of his were
published. Most of his ideas are still used by many scientists today. His name,
"Einstein," has become synonymous with genius.

COMPREHENSION QUESTIONS

Decide if each statement is true [T] or false [F]. If it is false, correct it.

1. [   ] Einstein developed the formula based on the research of scientists around the world.

2. [   ] He did not do well at school because he was deeply involved in physics.

3. [   ] Before he moved to the US, he received the Nobel Prize.

4. [   ] Einstein developed an atomic bomb with another Hungarian American physicist.

5. [   ] Einstein's suggestion was related to the bombs dropped on Hiroshima and Nagasaki.

Complete the outline notes below. You can look at the passage if you want.

PROFILE OF ALBERT EINSTEIN

1 Why famous?

- invented the most famous **1.** _____ : $E = mc^2$
  → an important **2.** _____ of science
- received the Nobel Prize in **3.** _____ in 1921

2 Who was he?

March 14, 1879	born into a Jewish family in **4.** _____
3 years old	started to speak
at school	did not work hard because the classes **5.** _____ him
	became interested in **6.** _____ rules of physics
1905	published the calculations for $E = mc^2$
1922	received the Nobel Prize

3 What did he do (after the Nobel Prize)?

after the prize	became a **7.** _____ at Princeton University in the US
1939	suggested the development of an atomic **8.** _____ to President Roosevelt
April 18, 1955	died in Princeton, New Jersey

✶ published more than 300 **9.** _____ works and over 150 non **9.** _____ work
  → "Einstein" means **10.** _____

THE GENIUS OF ALBERT EINSTEIN

UNIT 1
UNIT 2
UNIT 3
UNIT 4
UNIT 5
UNIT 6
UNIT 7
UNIT 8
UNIT 9
UNIT 10
UNIT 11
UNIT 12
UNIT 13
UNIT 14

WRITING AND DISCUSSION

Read the questions below and write down your ideas or opinions. Exchange your ideas or opinions with your classmates. Use the hints if you want.

1. Who has received a Nobel Prize before? What did he/she do? What was his/her life like?

   Hints ➡ Mother Teresa / helped sick people / built homes for orphans

   Your Ideas

   ....
   ....
   ....
   ....
   ....

2. Who is your favorite famous person? What did he/she do? Why do you like him/her?

   Hints ➡ broke several records / his/her music influences me / respect his/her motto

   Your Ideas

   ....
   ....
   ....
   ....
   ....

FURTHER STUDY

ActeaBo

For further study, access ActeaBo and review today's lesson.

http://acteabo.jp

Leonardo da Vinci

WARM-UP QUESTIONS

Discuss the questions below with your classmates.

1. What do you know about da Vinci?
2. Where can you see his famous paintings?

VOCABULARY 🖸 12

From the choices below, choose the word which fits best in each sentence.

1. We can _____ life as ongoing and dynamic education.
2. The _____ of the smartphone has revolutionized our daily life.
3. There is a plan to _____ a new building on campus.
4. This page shows a clear outline of a _____ for medical students.
5. The human body contains many _____ such as the heart and brain.
6. This document is for _____ use only and not to be distributed without permission.
7. This _____ helps readers understand the text.
8. Knowledge of _____ is useful for teaching yoga.
9. The patterns on either side of the door are perfectly_____.
10. He still has not been able to stop smoking as nicotine is _____ addictive.

anatomy	conceptualize	construct	diagram	incredibly
internal	invention	organs	skeleton	symmetrical

Learning vocabulary with prefixes and suffixes (2)

In addition to those introduced in Unit 5, here are some other common prefixes and suffixes. Knowing their meanings will surely help you remember more words more easily.

Example

prefixes:	en/m- (making verb)	con/m- (together)	re- (back)
e.g.	encourage empower	company connect	reward retire

suffixes:	-ize (making verb)	-scribe (write)	-ant/ent (person)
e.g.	specialize realize	transcribe describe	participant client

EXERCISE

Make a list of three unknown words from the passage on pp. 42-43. Then, check their meaning by analyzing the prefixes and suffixes. Share interesting or surprising ones with your classmates.

Unknown Words

↟ *The Last Supper* (1498)

READING PASSAGE 13

Read the passage below and analyze unknown words with prefixes and suffixes.

1   Leonardo da Vinci was an Italian scientist, botanist, anatomist, engineer, inventor, mathematician, architect, sculptor, musician, writer, and painter. He is widely regarded as one of the greatest painters of all time and the most talented polymath who ever lived. He was born in 1452 in Vinci, Italy, and
5 died in 1519.

2   As an engineer, da Vinci conceptualized many of our modern inventions, such as helicopters, tanks, calculators, and solar power. However, most of his inventions could not be constructed because the science of his time was not advanced
10 enough.

3   As an anatomist, da Vinci cut open human corpses and drew the human skeleton and its parts: muscles and sinews, sex organs, and various internal organs.

15 He recorded his studies of science and engineering in notebooks, leaving 13,000 pages of drawings, scientific diagrams, and ideas about the nature of painting. His studies about anatomy, art, and engineering are

↟ *Mona Lisa* (c. 1503–1506)

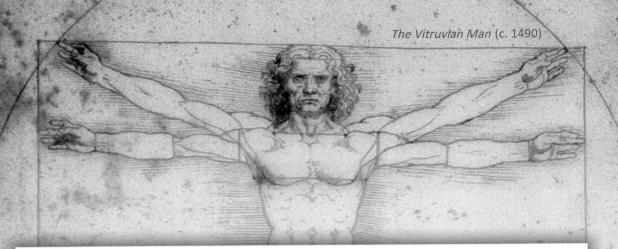

The Vitruvian Man (c. 1490)

20 brought together in his illustration, *The Vitruvian Man*. This illustration shows a beautifully detailed man moving his arms and legs in a symmetrical, realistic way. Because of his detailed study of human anatomy, da Vinci could create incredibly realistic drawings and paintings. His most famous paintings are the *Mona Lisa* and *The Last Supper*.

25 ❹   Da Vinci's father was a Florentine notary. His mother was a peasant woman or possibly a slave from the Middle East. When he was 14 years old, he went to work in the studio of a famous painter. It was there that he began to learn the skills he would master so completely.

❺   We know very little about da Vinci's life. Luckily, some of his work remains
30 behind to inspire us.

COMPREHENSION QUESTIONS

Decide if each statement is true [T] or false [F]. If it is false, correct it.

1. [   ] Da Vinci engaged in many different careers including scientist and botanist.

2. [   ] The science of da Vinci's time made it difficult to realize most of his ideas.

3. [   ] Da Vinci studied dead human bodies and made many drawings.

4. [   ] Some of da Vinci's paintings reflect his deep study of anatomy.

5. [   ] Da Vinci's parents were from a rich family.

Complete the outline notes below. You can look at the passage if you want.

PROFILE OF LEONARDO DA VINCI

1 Brief history

1452	born in Vinci, Italy
14 years old	went to 1. _____ in the studio and learned the skills of painting
1519	died

2 As an engineer

* conceptualized many modern 2. _____

    e.g.) helicopters, tanks, 3. _____, solar power, etc.

* but most of them were not 4. _____

3 As an anatomist

* analyzed the human body and drew its 5. _____, muscles, 6. _____, etc.
* recorded his studies on 13,000 pages of drawings, 7. _____ and ideas

4 As an artist

* created incredibly 8. _____ drawings and paintings

    e.g.) *Mona Lisa, The Last Supper*:

    his 9. _____ study of human anatomy

    The Vitruvian Man:

    his studies of anatomy, art, and engineering

    all 10. _____ together

WRITING AND DISCUSSION

Read the questions below and write down your ideas or opinions.
Exchange your ideas or opinions with your classmates. Use the hints
if you want.

1. What impressed you most about da Vinci?

> *Hints* ➡ brought together / human body /
> beyond science at that time

Your Ideas

....
....
....
....
....

2. Which historical person do you respect most? Why?

> *Hints* ➡ broke several records / his/her music influences me /
> respect his/her motto

Your Ideas

....
....
....
....
....

FURTHER STUDY

For further study, access ActeaBo and review today's lesson.

http://acteabo.jp

UNIT 1
UNIT 2
UNIT 3
UNIT 4
UNIT 5
UNIT 6 LEONARDO DA VINCI
UNIT 7
UNIT 8
UNIT 9
UNIT 10
UNIT 11
UNIT 12
UNIT 13
UNIT 14

Taiwan—Beware of Typhoons

WARM-UP QUESTIONS

Discuss the questions below with your classmates.

1. If you have a chance to visit Taiwan, what do you want to do there?

2. What do you think is the best season for overseas tourists to visit Japan?

VOCABULARY 🔘 14

From the choices below, choose the word which fits best in each sentence.

1. The city warns tourists to _____ of pickpockets in crowded places.

2. I have known Hanako for years. _____, I have known her since we were babies.

3. The children enjoyed trying to _____ the balloons by sitting on them.

4. Everyone was tired as the meeting _____ for a few hours without a break.

5. This year's low _____ has greatly affected farmers' crops.

6. He gave a good speech on the stage without _____ to his notes.

7. Blue areas _____ lakes or rivers on the map.

8. This author is famous for a _____ of novels based on the arts.

9. Fresh vegetables lose nutritional _____ during transport.

10. You will find a similar pattern in the _____ examples.

actually	beware	burst	following	lasted
rainfall	referring	represent	series	value

Making use of visual aids (1)

Visual aids, such as graphs, pie charts, and pictures, give you many hints about the story in a passage. Looking at them before reading the passage also helps activate your background knowledge.

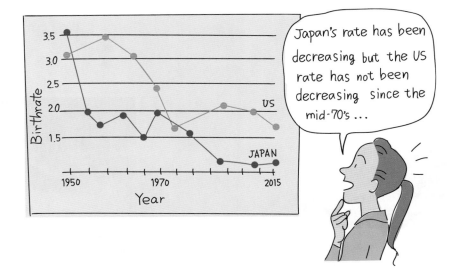

EXERCISE

Look at the bar graph below. What does it show? What does it compare? Also, link what you find in the graph with what you already know.

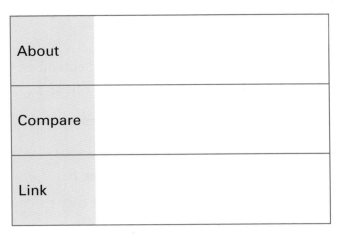

About	
Compare	
Link	

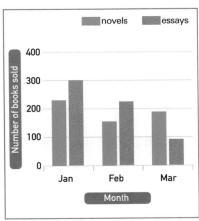

UNIT 1
UNIT 2
UNIT 3
UNIT 4
UNIT 5
UNIT 6
UNIT 7
UNIT 8
UNIT 9
UNIT 10
UNIT 11
UNIT 12
UNIT 13
UNIT 14

TAIWAN—BEWARE OF TYPHOONS

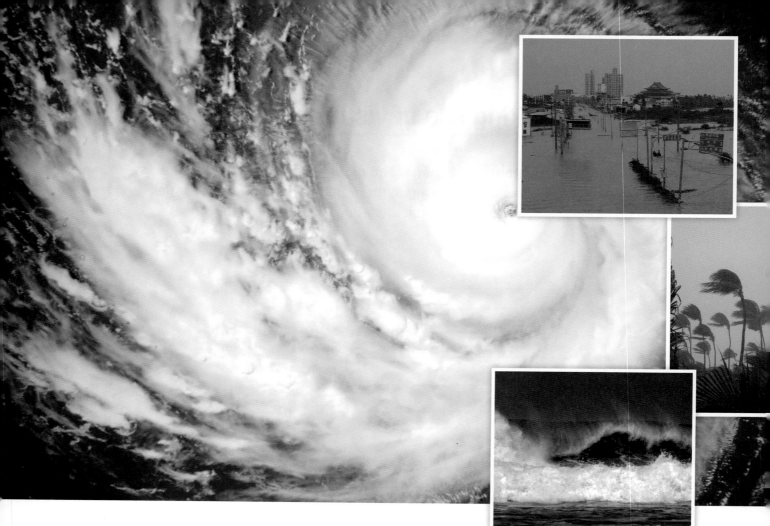

READING PASSAGE

CD 15

Read the passage below and predict the content from the graph.

1   If you are going to visit Taiwan, be sure to bring a pair of shorts, a T-shirt, and an umbrella. Actually, maybe it is better if you bring two umbrellas. It is always possible that the first one will be destroyed by a powerful burst of wind during a typhoon.

5 **2**   Taiwan has a typhoon season that generally lasts from July to September. These large tropical storms can be very dangerous. They often bring damaging winds and very heavy rain to this area. Everyone stays indoors whenever a typhoon passes over the island.

  3   For more detailed information on rainfall in Taiwan, refer to the bar
10 graph. A bar graph represents data using a series of bars, making it easy to compare different values. Use the bar graph to answer the following questions.

>> The weather in Taiwan is usually hot and humid with a lot of rainfall.

Average rainfall in in Tainan, Taiwan

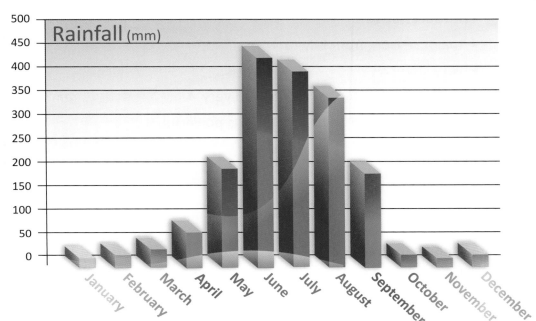

Rainfall (mm)

500	
450	
400	
350	
300	
250	
200	
150	
100	
50	
0	

January February March April May June July August September October November December

UNIT 1
UNIT 2
UNIT 3
UNIT 4
UNIT 5
UNIT 6
UNIT 7
UNIT 8
UNIT 9
UNIT 10
UNIT 11
UNIT 12
UNIT 13
UNIT 14

TAIWAN—BEWARE OF TYPHOONS

COMPREHENSION QUESTIONS

Decide if each statement is true [T] or false [F]. If it is false, correct it.

1. [   ] The writer advises carrying more than two umbrellas in Taiwan.
2. [   ] Bar graphs are useful in comparing values.
3. [   ] There is over 350 mm of rainfall in December in Taiwan.
4. [   ] There is less than 100 mm of rainfall in January in Taiwan.
5. [   ] Taiwan has more rainfall in October than in April.

Complete the outline notes below. You can look at the passage if you want.

TYPHOONS IN TAIWAN

1 Characteristics

- major season: from July to ___1.___
- very large ___2.___ storms
- bring ___3.___ winds and very ___4.___ rain
  - → umbrellas will be destroyed by a powerful ___5.___ of wind
  - → people stay ___6.___

2 Details

According to the ___7.___ graph:

- June has the highest ___8.___ ___9.___
- November has the ___10.___ ___8.___ ___9.___

WRITING AND DISCUSSION

Read the questions below and write down your ideas or opinions. Exchange your ideas or opinions with your classmates. Use the hints if you want.

1. What do you think visitors to Japan need to beware of? Why?

Hints ➡ earthquakes / snowstorm / humid

> **Your Ideas**
>
> ....
>
> ....
>
> ....
>
> ....

2. Based on your experiences of overseas trips/domestic tours, what do you recommend that your classmates take with them? Why?

Hints ➡ sunglasses / sunscreen / disposable warmers

> **Your Ideas**
>
> ....
>
> ....
>
> ....
>
> ....

FURTHER STUDY

For further study, access ActeaBo and review today's lesson.

http://acteabo.jp

UNIT 1
UNIT 2
UNIT 3
UNIT 4
UNIT 5
UNIT 6
UNIT 7
UNIT 8
UNIT 9
UNIT 10
UNIT 11
UNIT 12
UNIT 13
UNIT 14

TAIWAN—BEWARE OF TYPHOONS

Making use of visual aids

Pie Chart: Better Sundays Through Efficiency

WARM-UP QUESTIONS

Discuss the questions below with your classmates.

1. What kinds of charts do you see in your daily life?

2. Do you remember what you used to do when you were a child? Give some examples.

VOCABULARY 🎧 16

From the choices below, choose the word which fits best in each sentence.

1. I _____ that he would forgive her because of her sincere manner.

2. His files were very _____—he could not find anything he wanted.

3. People who live near the beach are _____ of the danger of sunbathing at midday.

4. She does not think the _____ truth has come out, but she wants to know what happened.

5. He has started practicing yoga as a way to _____ his stress.

6. He insists that of all insects, only _____ have these specialized fore-wings.

7. Some parents are too _____ with their children while others are too easy-going.

8. We were surprised when the emergency _____ of our phones sounded.

9. This _____ shows rice production in Japan.

10. She plans to _____ money to travel around Europe, but she does not know how to get a ticket.

alarm	assumed	aware	beetles	chart
disorganized	handle	spend	strict	whole

Making use of visual aids (2)

When you predict the contents of a passage from visual aids, guessing what words or phrases may appear in the passage will help you understand it. You can activate not only the background knowledge you already have but also your knowledge of vocabulary.

EXERCISE

Predict the content of the passage and the background information from the bar graph below. Also, list up the vocabulary related to the background information.

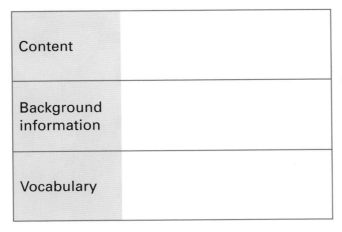

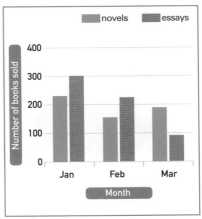

READING PASSAGE 17

Read the passage below using the pie chart on the next page.

1   People often assume that all kids are very disorganized, but that is not true. Take me for example. I work hard all week going to school, doing homework, practicing the piano, and doing chores around the house. I even walk our dog, Crispy, twice a day. My parents are aware of how hard I work

5 from Monday to Saturday, so they let me do whatever I want for seven hours and 15 minutes every Sunday.

2   That is a whole lot of free time for one kid to handle. A lot of other kids would waste most of it trying to decide what to do next. Should I climb a tree or go hunting for beetles? I am not one of those kids. I have drafted a strict

10 schedule for how to spend my Sunday afternoons. Once the time is up for one activity, an alarm on my watch will go off, and I will move on to the next one on the list. If you do not believe me, I have made a chart that shows how I like to spend my time on Sundays.

⩔ People often assume that all kids are very disorganized, but that is not true.

Free time

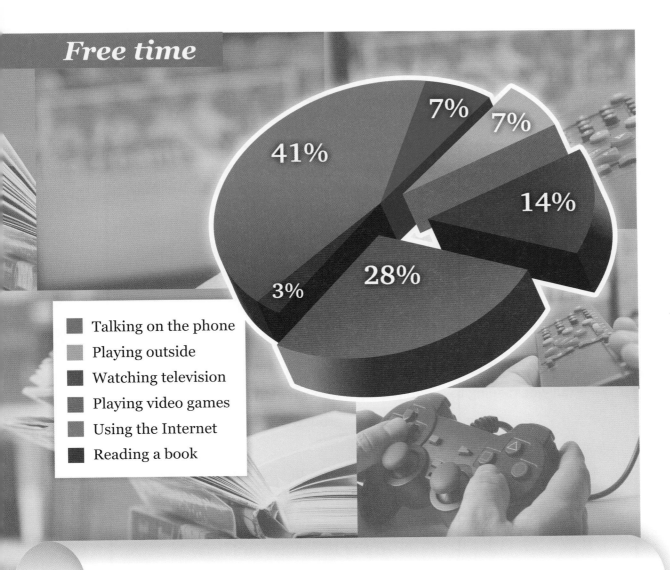

- Talking on the phone
- Playing outside
- Watching television
- Playing video games
- Using the Internet
- Reading a book

UNIT 1
UNIT 2
UNIT 3
UNIT 4
UNIT 5
UNIT 6
UNIT 7
UNIT 8
UNIT 9
UNIT 10
UNIT 11
UNIT 12
UNIT 13
UNIT 14

PIE CHART: BETTER SUNDAYS THROUGH EFFICIENCY

COMPREHENSION QUESTIONS

Decide if each statement is true [T] or false [F]. If it is false, correct it.

1. [   ] People often think that many children are very organized.

2. [   ] The author walks his/her dog, Crispy, once a day.

3. [   ] Many kids would waste their time by trying to decide what to do next.

4. [   ] When an alarm on his/her watch goes off, the kid moves on to the next activity.

5. [   ] The author has made a chart to explain how he/she spends his/her time on weekdays.

GRAPHIC SUMMARY

Complete the outline notes below. You can look at the passage if you want.

PIE CHART: BETTER SUNDAYS THROUGH EFFICIENCY

1 **The case of many kids**

- people think that kids are 1. _____
    ↓
    Not true! They work 2. _____
- waste time trying to decide what to do 3. _____

2 **The author's case**

- all week: going to school, doing homework, practicing the piano, doing 4. _____ around the house, walking a dog
    → his/her parents 5. _____ of how hard their kid works
    → let him/her do 6. _____ he/she wants for 7. _____ hours and 15 minutes on Sunday
- draft a 8. _____ schedule on Sunday afternoons
    → time up for one activity
    → 9. _____ on to the next one on the list
- a 10. _____ shows how he/she spends his/her time on Sundays

WRITING AND DISCUSSION

Read the questions below and write down your ideas or opinions. Exchange your ideas or opinions with your classmates. Use the hints if you want.

1. What is your schedule like on weekdays? Explain it.

Hints ➡ social activities / travel to school / cleaning my room

> **Your Ideas**
>
> ....
>
> ....
>
> ....
>
> ....

2. How do you organize your free time efficiently?

Hints ➡ make a list / use cell phone's alarm

> **Your Ideas**
>
> ....
>
> ....
>
> ....
>
> ....

FURTHER STUDY

For further study, access ActeaBo and review today's lesson.

http://acteabo.jp

Global Warming

WARM-UP QUESTIONS

Discuss the questions below with your classmates.

1. What kinds of environmental problems are happening in the world?
2. What problems do you think global warming causes?

VOCABULARY   18

From the choices below, choose the word which fits best in each sentence.

1. Most stalkers act unpredictably and _____ their victims.
2. Some vehicles use two kinds of _____, that is, gasoline and diesel.
3. The man was _____ from prison after two years.
4. _____ have risen over the past few years.
5. This is one of the worst natural _____ that has ever occurred in the country.
6. Severe _____ has ruined the crops this year.
7. We have to _____ our plans to fit the manager's timetable.
8. The ice began to _____ when the sun came out.
9. Nobody can _____ what will happen next year.
10. Sorghum is a cash crop that can be used as a _____ source of energy.

adapt	disasters	drought	fuel	melt
predict	released	renewable	temperatures	threaten

Slash reading (1)

When you read a difficult passage, you may have to reread some sentences a few times to get the meaning. How can you solve this "rereading" problem? One way is to put slashes between "meaningful chunks."

Example

I want to visit / Italy, Sweden, and the U.K. / because / my friends live there. / I am working part time in an *izakaya* / to save money / for my trip. / I am very excited / about traveling overseas.

EXERCISE

Read the sentence below. Try to put slashes between the meaningful chunks. Check them with your partner and teacher.

If you are interested in the environmental issues, the first thing you need to do is to find an organization that can provide you with plenty of opportunities to make a contribution in that field.

UNIT 1
UNIT 2
UNIT 3
UNIT 4
UNIT 5
UNIT 6
UNIT 7
UNIT 8
UNIT 9 GLOBAL WARMING
UNIT 10
UNIT 11
UNIT 12
UNIT 13
UNIT 14

Global warming increases the chances of many types of disasters.

⌄ Hurricanes

READING PASSAGE 19

Read the passage below and add slashes where appropriate.

1   There is an environmental crisis that is threatening the planet. It is called "the greenhouse effect" or "global warming." The problem comes from fossil fuels such as natural gas, oil, and coal. When countries burn these fuels for energy, they release carbon dioxide (CO_2) and other dangerous "greenhouse
5 gases" into the atmosphere. These gases prevent heat from escaping into outer space. They are like a blanket that is causing both land and sea temperatures to rise.

2   Global warming is a lot more serious than a few more days of hot weather every year. As the planet heats up, the balance of nature begins to change. This
10 increases the chances of many types of natural disasters, such as hurricanes, floods, and drought. It is difficult for plant and animal life to adapt to hotter temperatures, so global warming threatens our crops and the survival of certain species as well.

3   One of the most dangerous
15 consequences of global warming is the huge amounts of ice in the Arctic and Antarctic regions that have started to melt. The melting of this polar ice causes
20 worldwide sea levels to rise,

⌃ Governments around the world have started focusing on developing renewable energy sources.

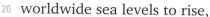

Floods

Droughts

UNIT 1
UNIT 2
UNIT 3
UNIT 4
UNIT 5
UNIT 6
UNIT 7
UNIT 8
UNIT 9 GLOBAL WARMING
UNIT 10
UNIT 11
UNIT 12
UNIT 13
UNIT 14

threatening people who live in low-lying countries like Bangladesh. In fact, some reports predict that countries like the small Pacific island of Tuvalu could be completely underwater by the year 2100.

4   The good news is that there is something we can do to fight global
25 warming. We must use less fossil fuel. Governments around the world have begun to focus on renewable energy sources such as wind, geothermal, water, and solar power. Many individuals have also made positive steps by improving their personal habits. Some have purchased electric cars and others have sold their cars altogether.

30 5   However, there is a long way to go before global warming is solved. Unfortunately, many people around the world still do not take the problem very seriously.

COMPREHENSION QUESTIONS

Decide if each statement is true [T] or false [F]. If it is false, correct it.

1. [   ] Released gases like CO_2 stop heat from escaping into space.

2. [   ] Global warming can cause more serious problems than a few additional days of hot weather every year.

3. [   ] The balance of nature begins to change when the planet heats up.

4. [   ] The people who live in low-lying area in Bangladesh are threatened due to melting ice.

5. [   ] Many individuals have made positive steps by keeping their personal habits.

Complete the outline notes below. You can look at the passage if you want.

GLOBAL WARMING

1 General information

- global warming = "the 1. _____ effect"
- caused by fossil 2. _____
  when burned, 3. _____ and other dangerous gases

- changes the balance of nature
  → increases 4. _____ such as hurricanes, floods, and drought
  → makes it more difficult for plant and animal life to 5. _____

2 Consequences

- the huge amounts of 6. _____ started to melt
  → worldwide sea levels to 7. _____
  e.g.) the small Pacific island of Tuvalu:
      8. _____ by the year 2100

3 Good news

- governments: focus on 9. _____ energy sources
- individuals: use less fossil fuel
  e.g.) buying electric cars and selling cars
- ＊ many people still do not 10. _____ the problem very seriously

WRITING AND DISCUSSION

Read the questions below and write down your ideas or opinions.
Exchange your ideas or opinions with your classmates. Use the hints
if you want.

1. What are the effects of global warming on your daily life?
Give some examples.

Hints ➲ increase the cost of food / get too hot

> **Your Ideas**
>
> ....
>
> ....
>
> ....
>
> ....

2. To stop global warming, what can we do?

Hints ➲ use electric cars / sell our cars /
not use air conditioners

> **Your Ideas**
>
> ....
>
> ....
>
> ....
>
> ....

FURTHER STUDY

For further study, access ActeaBo and review today's lesson.

http://acteabo.jp

Avoiding Cancer

WARM-UP QUESTIONS

Discuss the questions below with your classmates.

1. What do you think the most terrible diseases in the world are?
2. What types of cancer are there in the world? Give some examples.

VOCABULARY 🔘 20

From the choices below, choose the word which fits best in each sentence.

1. He is suffering from heart _____.
2. Heart _____ has a complex structure that includes blood vessels.
3. The population of endangered species has been _____ for decades.
4. An inspection revealed that the mine _____ both the air and the groundwater.
5. She has _____ headaches when she takes a bus.
6. She always tries to exercise and eat _____ food.
7. There is still no _____ for AIDS.
8. The government has reformed the _____ insurance system.
9. It is important to _____ a constant temperature inside the greenhouse.
10. Research has shown the benefits of a vegetarian _____.

cure	diet	disease	dwindling	frequent
healthy	maintain	medical	polluted	tissue

Slash reading (2)

There are several rules for putting slashes (/) between each meaningful chunk while reading a passage. By paying attention to these rules, you can understand the passage more easily and quickly.

You put a slash ...

1. after a comma (,) and a period (.)

2. before verbs (to separate them from subjects)

3. before and after the objects of transitive verbs (e.g. created / a huge amount of employment in the area)

4. after collocations (e.g. "regard A as B" and "consider A to be B")

5. before relative clauses (e.g. the milk / I could not finish drinking)

6. before and after prepositional phrases (e.g.: in, on, to, during, by)

7. before conjunctions (e.g. and, because, if)

Example

I / am learning / English / to study in the U.K., / because it has the most advanced medical system / in the world. / My dream is / to learn / their system / and use the knowledge / that I gain there / for my home country, / Japan. /

EXERCISE

Put slashes for meaningful chunks in the sentences in the first paragraph of the passage on p.66. Then, read them aloud with your partner.

Student 1: Read the first chunk aloud (to the first slash).

Student 2: Listen to Student 1's reading and repeat it without looking at the passage.

Student 1: Read the next chunk aloud (to the next slash).

Student 2: Listen to Student 1's reading and repeat it without looking at the passage again.

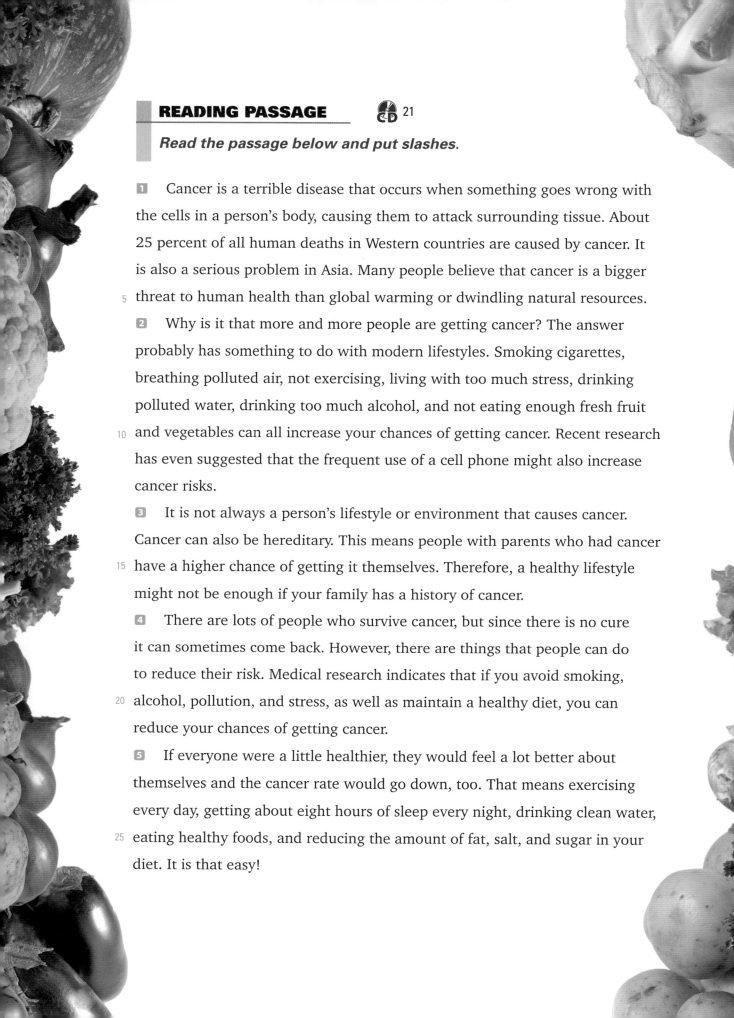

READING PASSAGE 🎧 21

Read the passage below and put slashes.

1   Cancer is a terrible disease that occurs when something goes wrong with the cells in a person's body, causing them to attack surrounding tissue. About 25 percent of all human deaths in Western countries are caused by cancer. It is also a serious problem in Asia. Many people believe that cancer is a bigger
5 threat to human health than global warming or dwindling natural resources.

2   Why is it that more and more people are getting cancer? The answer probably has something to do with modern lifestyles. Smoking cigarettes, breathing polluted air, not exercising, living with too much stress, drinking polluted water, drinking too much alcohol, and not eating enough fresh fruit
10 and vegetables can all increase your chances of getting cancer. Recent research has even suggested that the frequent use of a cell phone might also increase cancer risks.

3   It is not always a person's lifestyle or environment that causes cancer. Cancer can also be hereditary. This means people with parents who had cancer
15 have a higher chance of getting it themselves. Therefore, a healthy lifestyle might not be enough if your family has a history of cancer.

4   There are lots of people who survive cancer, but since there is no cure it can sometimes come back. However, there are things that people can do to reduce their risk. Medical research indicates that if you avoid smoking,
20 alcohol, pollution, and stress, as well as maintain a healthy diet, you can reduce your chances of getting cancer.

5   If everyone were a little healthier, they would feel a lot better about themselves and the cancer rate would go down, too. That means exercising every day, getting about eight hours of sleep every night, drinking clean water,
25 eating healthy foods, and reducing the amount of fat, salt, and sugar in your diet. It is that easy!

Ways to reduce your risk of cancer

UNIT 1
UNIT 2
UNIT 3
UNIT 4
UNIT 5
UNIT 6
UNIT 7
UNIT 8
UNIT 9
UNIT 10
AVOIDING CANCER
UNIT 11
UNIT 12
UNIT 13
UNIT 14

Exercise regularly.

Eat a plant-based diet.

Avoid alcohol.

Do not smoke.

COMPREHENSION QUESTIONS

Decide if each statement is true [T] or false [F]. If it is false, correct it.

1. [　] Many people believe that cancer is a more serious problem than global warming.

2. [　] Our modern lifestyle is one of the reasons that people get cancer.

3. [　] Cancer can be hereditary, but the chances of getting it are very low.

4. [　] Because there is a cure for cancer, there are many people who survive the disease.

5. [　] If people exercise regularly, sleep well, and eat healthy foods, they are less likely to get cancer.

GRAPHIC SUMMARY

Complete the outline notes below. You can look at the passage if you want.

AVOIDING CANCER

1 General information
- causes cells to attack surrounding ⬚ 1.
- causes about ⬚ 2. % of human deaths in Western countries

2 Causes of cancer: Modern lifestyles
- more risks

  e.g.) ⬚ 3. , breathing ⬚ 4. air,
  not exercising, living with stress, drinking polluted water
  and ⬚ 5. , not eating fresh fruit and
  ⬚ 6.
  frequent use of a ⬚ 7.

3 Cause of cancer: Hereditary
- people with ⬚ 8. who had cancer
  → higher chance of cancer
- a ⬚ 9. lifestyle might not be enough

4 To reduce cancer risk
- avoiding smoking, alcohol, pollution, and stress
- to ⬚ 10. a healthy diet

WRITING AND DISCUSSION

Read the questions below and write down your ideas or opinions.
Exchange your ideas or opinions with your classmates. Use the hints
if you want.

1. Do you have any bad lifestyle habits?

Hints ➲ eat too much / do not exercise / stay up late

Your Ideas

....
....
....
....
....

2. What would you do if you got a serious disease?

Hints ➲ search for a good doctor / try any cure /
do what I want to do

Your Ideas

....
....
....
....
....

FURTHER STUDY

ActeaBo

For further study, access ActeaBo and review today's lesson.

http://acteabo.jp

Obesity

WARM-UP QUESTIONS

Discuss the questions below with your classmates.

1. What dishes do you usually cook when your friends visit you for dinner?
2. What do you think of online food delivery services?

VOCABULARY 🄲🄳 22

From the choices below, choose the word which fits best in each sentence.

1. Controlling your weight is important for reducing risks of cancer and _____.

2. Gun violence is one of the _____ of my daughter's generation.

3. My luggage was _____ by five kilos.

4. In debate class, the teacher tries to get all of us to _____.

5. Exercise helps _____ the risk of heart disease.

6. I saw a look of _____ in my son's eyes before his birthday.

7. I consumed an _____ amount of coffee yesterday and I could not sleep until late at night.

8. Young elephants must eat several times daily, or they will _____ to death.

9. People on low-calorie diets sometimes end up getting poor _____.

10. Caffeine in coffee is _____ and some people cannot stop drinking it.

addictive	contribute	excessive	expectancy	nutrition
obesity	overweight	reduce	scourges	starve

Scanning (1)

You may have experienced the feeling of getting lost while reading a passage in English. In this situation, scanning is useful. Scanning is reading to find the important information first. You can effectively scan the passage by making use of keywords from the comprehension questions. These keywords contain important information about the passage: who, what, when, where, why, and how (5W1H).

Example   Why did Aya first become interested in changing her
               why   who   how
               diet and lifestyle?
                    what

EXERCISE
Try to pick up keywords from the questions below and circle them.
Check them with your partner and the teacher.

Questions
a) According to the research, what does obesity cause?
b) How was obesity considered in the past and why was that?
c) Why is obesity so expensive for societies?

READING PASSAGE 🎧 23

Read the passage below using the comprehension questions.

⌄ Obesity is the scourge of the 21st century.

1   Doctors say that obesity is the scourge of the 21st century. But what is obesity?

2   A person who is obese is too heavy. The problem of being
5 overweight is caused by an excessive accumulation of fat. Research shows that obesity may cause or contribute to various diseases, such as cardiovascular diseases, sleep
10 apnea, certain types of cancer, gout, and osteoarthritis. Obesity has also been found to reduce a person's life expectancy.

3   A person's "BMI" (body mass index) can show if a person is obese. BMI is calculated by dividing an
15 individual's weight in kilograms by the square of his or her height in meters. Someone who weighs 80 kilograms and is 1.6 meters tall will have a BMI of 31.25. A BMI of between 18.5 and 24 is said to be healthy. If it is more than 30, the person is probably obese.

4   In the past, it was considered beautiful to be heavy, because it meant you
20 had enough food. Now, obesity has become a serious public health problem. Between the 1980s and today, the number of obese people in the United

≫ Junk food makes us tired.

UNIT 1

UNIT 2

UNIT 3

UNIT 4

UNIT 5

UNIT 6

UNIT 7

UNIT 8

UNIT 9

UNIT 10

OBESITY

UNIT 11

UNIT 12

UNIT 13

UNIT 14

States has jumped. For the first time in human history, there are now more overweight people than people who are starving. Obese people may need medical care more often than people with a healthy weight, so obesity is very

25 expensive for societies.

5 Why are so many people obese? There are many reasons, but generally, we eat too much food and do not exercise enough. The types of food we eat also have an impact. Sugary, processed foods

30 give us a rush without actually providing much nutrition. They can also be addictive. It is also hard to exercise when the junk food we eat does not give us energy and makes us tired.

6 But we can take control. As individuals and

35 societies, we should take a hard look at our choices and make some changes.

COMPREHENSION QUESTIONS

Decide if each statement is true [T] or false [F]. If it is false, correct it.

1. [   ] Obesity is the problem of being overweight.

2. [   ] Research concludes that obesity causes and contributes to various diseases.

3. [   ] A BMI of less than 30 shows that a person may be obese.

4. [   ] Compared to the past, obesity in modern society has a different meaning.

5. [   ] Sugary, processed foods provide us with a rush as well as nutrition.

Complete the outline notes below. You can look at the passage if you want.

OBESITY

1 Obesity

- the scourge of the 1. _____ century
- caused by an 2. _____ accumulation of fat
- leads to various diseases

    e.g.) cardiovascular disease, sleep apnea, 3. _____ ,
        gout, and osteoarthritis

- reduce life 4. _____

2 BMI

- = Body Mass Index
- can show if a person is 5. _____

    = an individual's 6. _____ ÷(height × height)

    → healthy = 18.5 – 24

        obese = more than 7. _____

3 Past vs. Now

- past:

    heavy = 8. _____ ← having enough food

- now:

    obesity = serious public health problem

        = expensive for societies ← we eat too much food and do

            not 9. _____ enough

        food = much 10. _____ and addictive

→ We should take a hard look at our choices and make some changes.

WRITING AND DISCUSSION

Read the questions below and write down your ideas or opinions. Exchange your ideas or opinions with your classmates. Use the hints if you want.

1. Comparing the past with now, how has food service changed?

Hints ➡ online service / delivery service / convenience stores

> **Your Ideas**
>
> ....
>
> ....
>
> ....
>
> ....

2. What can you do to prevent obesity?

Hints ➡ exercise or go jogging / eat less salty food / check my BMI

> **Your Ideas**
>
> ....
>
> ....
>
> ....
>
> ....

FURTHER STUDY

For further study, access ActeaBo and review today's lesson.

http://acteabo.jp

UNIT 1
UNIT 2
UNIT 3
UNIT 4
UNIT 5
UNIT 6
UNIT 7
UNIT 8
UNIT 9
UNIT 10
OBESITY UNIT 11
UNIT 12
UNIT 13
UNIT 14

Democracy in the Modern World

WARM-UP QUESTIONS

Discuss the questions below with your classmates.

1. Do you keep up with political news in your country? Why or why not?
2. Which countries are democracies?

VOCABULARY 🎧 24

From the choices below, choose the word which fits best in each sentence.

1. They use _____ as a method of selecting representatives.
2. The members _____ him to be the leader of the group.
3. Each person in the community has a _____ to control their behavior.
4. In college, you have the _____ to do what you want.
5. This change has the _____ to impact our customers.
6. Unfortunately, hard work does not always _____ success.
7. The _____ has finally passed the budget for the next financial year.
8. The teacher always tells her students to be _____ and kind to their friends.
9. She is trying to _____ her English writing skills to pass the exam.
10. The woman works hard and _____ a little bit of quality time to relax.

democracy	deserves	elected	freedom	guarantee
improve	legislature	potential	responsibility	thoughtful

Scanning (2)

You may not find always the same keywords in the comprehension questions as in the passage. Another way of scanning is looking for synonyms. A synonym is a word or a phrase that means exactly or nearly the same as another word or phrase.

Example

Comprehension question: Why doesn't democracy <u>always offer</u> good government?

synonyms

Sentence: Having a democracy does not <u>guarantee</u> that the leaders of the government will do good things.

always offer
≒ guarantee

EXERCISE

Find the synonyms from the question and the part of the passage below, and highlight them.

> Question: How can democracies develop themselves?
> Part of the passage: ... A democracy also needs to grow and change in order to improve itself. ...

READING PASSAGE 25

Read the passage below and pay attention to the keywords in the comprehension questions and their synonyms in the passage.

1   Do you know what "democracy" is about? A democracy has leaders who are elected by the people in a particular area through voting. The government belongs to all the people, not to any king, dictator, or small group. Democracy is based on the idea that citizens have the power and responsibility to select

5 new leaders if the old leaders are not doing a good job. If there is freedom of speech and freedom of the press in a democratic country, each citizen can be informed about the potential leaders and can vote wisely.

2   Taiwan is a democracy. So are the United States, the United Kingdom, and many other countries in the world. Currently, there are about 123 countries

10 that say they have democratically elected leaders. Unfortunately, some countries that claim to be democratic are not in fact democracies.

3   Having a democracy does not guarantee that the leaders of the government will do good things. During the years leaders are in power, they may decide to do bad things and the citizens may have a limited ability to

15 stop them. The courts, legislature, or free press can often limit the damage

Democratic freedoms include the freedom of speech.

The establishment of universal male suffrage in France in 1848 was an important milestone in the history of democracy.

UNIT 1
UNIT 2
UNIT 3
UNIT 4
UNIT 5
UNIT 6
UNIT 7
UNIT 8
UNIT 9
UNIT 10
UNIT 11
UNIT 12
UNIT 13
UNIT 14

DEMOCRACY IN THE MODERN WORLD

being done by a bad leader. A democracy needs many honest and wise leaders as well as an educated and thoughtful population. A democracy also needs to
20 grow and change in order to improve itself. Examples of mature and strong democracies can be found in Europe, North America, Australia, and New Zealand.
25 ❹ An open and honest democracy is what most of the people in the world desire. Despite lies that may be told by bad leaders, people all over the world will continue to struggle for the healthy
30 democracies that they deserve.

COMPREHENSION QUESTIONS

Decide if each statement is true [T] or false [F]. If it is false, correct it.

1. [　] The government of a democracy belongs to all the nations, not to any king or dictator.

2. [　] Freedom of speech and freedom of the press make it less possible for people to choose their leaders wisely.

3. [　] A democracy guarantees that the leaders will do good things for all citizens.

4. [　] Not only honest and wise leaders, but also educated and thoughtful people are needed in a democracy.

5. [　] Europe, North America, Australia, and New Zealand have mature and strong democracies.

Complete the outline notes below. You can look at the passage if you want.

DEMOCRACY IN THE MODERN WORLD

1 General information

- leaders are elected by 1. _____
- citizens have the 2. _____ and 3. _____ to select new leaders
- about 4. _____ countries are democracies ⇔ some countries are actually not

2 Limited power

- democracy ≠ the leader will do good things
- citizens have a 5. _____ ability to stop the leaders
  → the courts, 6. _____, or free press can limit the 7. _____

3 Needs

- honest and wise leaders
- 8. _____ and thoughtful people
- to grow and change to become 9. _____ and strong democracies

  → an 10. _____ and honest democracy

WRITING AND DISCUSSION

Read the questions below and write down your ideas or opinions. Exchange your ideas or opinions with your classmates. Use the hints if you want.

1. If you joined a group like a tennis club, how would you decide what the group does?

    Hints ➲ vote / leader's power / meetings

    > **Your Ideas**
    >
    > ....
    >
    > ....
    >
    > ....
    >
    > ....

2. What would happen if your community did not have democracy?

    Hints ➲ dictatorship / leave the community /
    cannot suggest anything

    > **Your Ideas**
    >
    > ....
    >
    > ....
    >
    > ....
    >
    > ....

FURTHER STUDY

For further study, access ActeaBo and review today's lesson.

http://acteabo.jp

UNIT 1
UNIT 2
UNIT 3
UNIT 4
UNIT 5
UNIT 6
UNIT 7
UNIT 8
UNIT 9
UNIT 10
UNIT 11
UNIT 12
UNIT 13
UNIT 14

DEMOCRACY IN THE MODERN WORLD

Borrowing From a Living Library

WARM-UP QUESTIONS

Discuss the questions below with your classmates.

1. What kinds of books do you often read? Why?

2. What was the most terrible experience in your life?

VOCABULARY 🎧 26

From the choices below, choose the word which fits best in each sentence.

1. The military force controlled the countryside and they _____ the towns.

2. Many people did not support her because their racial _____ was too strong.

3. It is important to make yourself accustomed to pain and danger without _____.

4. The appeal of the new sport _____ beyond the nation's boundaries.

5. He got many _____ responses to his presentation and was very happy.

6. They need to know that they should sort and classify things to _____ the information.

7. She is a _____ modern player and has great technical ability.

8. The woman explains why men are more likely to become _____ when drunk.

9. The long cold winter had only increased her _____ of the place.

10. We believe it will increase _____ for musicians and other artists to perform.

aggressive	conquered	fear	hatred	opportunities
organize	positive	prejudice	spread	typical

Paying attention to topic sentences (1)

How do you get the key points of a passage? If you read all of the sentences, it will take time. However, in the case of an explanatory passage, you can understand the important points more easily by reading the topic sentence of each paragraph.

If you connect all of the topic sentences, you will find it easy to understand the main idea of the passage. The topic sentence is usually the first or the last sentence of each paragraph.

Example

Do you know what a Boxbot, Flipper, or Thwackbot is? They are types of robots that are built to fight one another on television. BattleBots is an American company that hosts these robot competitions. It is also the name of a robot-fighting television program. Robot-fighting programs like *BattleBots* and *Robot Wars* have become popular all over the world. Millions of fans watch these programs.

Teams of engineers design and build robots that can cost up to US$50,000 and enter them into those television contests. They give their machines scary or silly names like Vlad the Impaler, The Judge, and Cereal Box Killer. In a BattleBots competition, competitors bring remote-controlled, armored robots armed with weapons and put them into an arena to do their best to destroy each other. There are no limits to how the robots can battle each other.

EXERCISE

Highlight the topic sentences of the first two paragraphs of the passage on p. 84.

UNIT 1
UNIT 2
UNIT 3
UNIT 4
UNIT 5
UNIT 6
UNIT 7
UNIT 8
UNIT 9
UNIT 10
UNIT 11
UNIT 12
UNIT 13
UNIT 14
BORROWING FROM A LIVING LIBRARY

READING PASSAGE 27

Read the passage below. Highlight the topic sentences to understand the main idea.

⌃ Stop the Violence logo

1 The world is full of different people who have lived very different lives. Some are rich, and others are poor. Some have conquered violence and hatred; others have never known fear. We all have our own story, but what is the best way to tell this story to another person? You
5 could write it down in a book, or better yet, go and tell them face-to-face. This is the idea behind the Human Library.

2 The story of the Human Library began at the Roskilde music festival in Denmark in 2000. That is where a nongovernment youth organization called Stop the Violence set up a small tent in order to spread their antiviolence
10 message. They believed that people could better understand strangers with different backgrounds if they had a face-to-face discussion about their experiences in life. At the time, there were over 75 "books" available, including policemen, politicians, graffiti artists, feminists, and soccer fans. The crowd's response at the festival was so positive that Stop the Violence decided
15 to expand the program overseas.

3 Now there are over 45 Human Libraries all over the world and they are all organized by the Human Library Organization in Denmark. These libraries are

« At the time, there were over 75 "books" available in the Human Library.

84

run by Human Library organizers who are responsible for collecting books and

20 lending them out to the public.

Human Library logo

❹ A typical book catalog will include general characteristics about the person, or "book," that is being offered. For example, there might be

25 a book called "Muslim" that lists the following characteristics: extremist, fundamentalist, aggressive terrorist. These are all popular prejudices against Muslims. In other words, they are

30 characteristics that people wrongly believe that every Muslim has. By listing these prejudices and giving people an opportunity to meet a real Muslim,

the Human Library is trying to challenge the way people see other groups in

35 society.

COMPREHENSION QUESTIONS

Decide if each statement is true [T] or false [F]. If it is false, correct it.

1. [   ] There are some people who have overcome violence and hatred.

2. [   ] A nongovernment youth organization in Denmark started to spread an antiviolence message.

3. [   ] Nowadays, there are over 75 "books" available, including policemen, politicians, and so on.

4. [   ] Stop the Violence decided not to expand their program because of the people's negative response.

5. [   ] Muslims are typically believed to be extremist, fundamentalist, and aggressive terrorists.

85

Complete the outline notes below. You can look at the passage if you want.

BORROWING FROM A LIVING LIBRARY

1 The idea of the Human Library

- full of **1.** [_____] people in the world
- all have our own story → better to tell in face-to-face
  → Human Library

2 The Origin

- Roskilde music festival in **2** [_____] in 2000
- Stop the **3.** [_____] : **4.** [_____] their antiviolence message
- a **5.** [_____] discussion = better understanding of **6.** [_____] with different backgrounds

3 Now

- over **7.** [_____] Human Libraries all over the world
- by the Human Library Organization in Denmark
  → responsible for **8.** [_____] and lending books

4 How to borrow a "book"

- a "book" catalogue with a list of general **9.** [_____] about the person (= "book")
  e.g.) a "Muslim" book
    = extremist, fundamentalist, aggressive terrorists
    = popular **10.** [_____] against them

- borrow a "book" = opportunity to meet a real Muslim
    = opportunity to change people's ways of seeing others

WRITING AND DISCUSSION

Read the questions below and write down your ideas or opinions. Exchange your ideas or opinions with your classmates. Use the hints if you want.

1. Do you want to use the Human Library? Why or why not?

Hints ➲ get information / think about life / face-to-face

Your Ideas

....

....

....

....

....

2. If you could borrow a book from the Human Library, what kind of book would you want to read?

Hints ➲ different environment / the same age as me / learn about how they live

Your Ideas

....

....

....

....

....

FURTHER STUDY
ActeaBo

For further study, access ActeaBo and review today's lesson.

http://acteabo.jp

UNIT **14**

Paying attention to topic sentences

The Importance of Language

WARM-UP QUESTIONS

Discuss the questions below with your classmates.

1. In what situations did you use language this morning?

2. What language did Japanese originate from?

VOCABULARY CD 28

From the choices below, choose the word which fits best in each sentence.

1. My father bought a set of _____ for my mother to use when gardening.

2. Computers are one of the benefits of modern _____.

3. One old blanket is not much help when trying to _____ in the wilderness.

4. We watched until our father completely _____ around the corner.

5. Rome is famous for its _____ historical buildings.

6. What kinds of _____ species once existed in Japan?

7. They _____ from a common ancestor but their appearances are quite different.

8. He did not understand my Japanese, so we held a simple _____ in English.

9. He has skills, knowledge, and the _____ to work anywhere in the world.

10. At that point the players were in a good mood and _____ with each other.

ability	ancient	civilization	conversation	cooperated
disappeared	evolved	extinct	survive	tools

Paying attention to topic sentences (2)

You may not always understand the topic sentences perfectly. When that happens, pick up a few keywords from each topic sentence. By connecting all of the keywords together, you can still get the gist of the passage.

Example

keywords   word you do not understand

1 Do you know what the largest flying bird is? It is the albatross. .....
?
....

2 An albatross's diet consists of squid, fish, and other small sea
?   ?
animals. ....

3 Some scientists believe that albatross couples perform special
?
dances together in order to make their relationship last longer. ....
?
....

4 When they fly, albatrosses use their long wings to glide through
?
air that is rising. ....

5 Albatrosses are currently threatened with extinction because of
?   ?
several factors. ....

EXERCISE

Read the first two paragraphs of the passage on p. 90. From their topic sentences, pick up a few keywords and try to understand the beginning of the story.

UNIT 1
UNIT 2
UNIT 3
UNIT 4
UNIT 5
UNIT 6
UNIT 7
UNIT 8
UNIT 9
UNIT 10
UNIT 11
UNIT 12
UNIT 13
UNIT 14

THE IMPORTANCE OF LANGUAGE

89

Cuneiform is the first known form of written language.

READING PASSAGE 29

Read the passage below and highlight topic sentences. If you do not understand them perfectly, connect the keywords from them.

1   Language is not just used for talking. It is our most important communication tool. Through language, we can tell other people what we think, how we feel, and what we need. Civilization itself depends on our ability to communicate.

5 **2**   Nobody knows exactly when people first started using language. Some scientists say that people first spoke to one another about two million years ago, while others say that the use of human language occurred only about 50,000 years ago.

3   Languages survive, grow, disappear, move from place to place, and change 10 with time. Some languages are ancient; others are new. There are nearly 7,000 different living languages around the world today (though there are many different ways to count languages). Many thousands more are already extinct. These languages all sound different, but they are thought to have come from a single ancient language. English, for example, originally evolved out of the 15 ancient Germanic language. This ancient Germanic language evolved into three types, West Germanic, East Germanic, and North Germanic.

>> English is the most obvious example of a lingua franca.

DO YOU SPEAK ENGLISH?

UNIT 1
UNIT 2
UNIT 3
UNIT 4
UNIT 5
UNIT 6
UNIT 7
UNIT 8
UNIT 9
UNIT 10
UNIT 11
UNIT 12
UNIT 13
UNIT 14

From West Germanic came Old English, and then over time, today's modern English.

4 20 Today, languages are used not only for conversation, but also in the magazines, books, and movies that fill our libraries and bookstores. The long stories we can tell separate us from the rest of the great apes.

5 Throughout history, many languages have served as a lingua franca—a common language that could be used as a bridge between 25 people of different cultures. Today, English is the main language that plays that role around the world. Over two billion people have some ability to use English. Most of these people have studied English as a second or third language.

6 Language helps people to cooperate, share knowledge, and 30 build up modern societies. The development of humanity's many languages was an important process that helped humans create their civilizations.

COMPREHENSION QUESTIONS

Decide if each statement is true [T] or false [F]. If it is false, correct it.

1. [   ] We can tell other people our ideas, feelings, and needs without language.

2. [   ] Most scientists say people first used language about two million years ago.

3. [   ] We count living languages in the world in many different ways.

4. [   ] The Germanic language changed into four types, West, East, North, and South Germanic.

5. [   ] A common language was used as a bridge to connect people of different cultures.

Complete the outline notes below. You can look at the passage if you want.

THE IMPORTANCE OF LANGUAGE

1 **Role of language**

- most important communication **1.** _____
- **2.** _____ depends on our ability to communicate

2 **Survive and disappear**

- **3.** _____ knows when people first started using language
- nearly **4.** _____ different living languages
  → from a single **5.** _____ language

e.g.) English has evolved out of the old **6.** _____

　　＊ many thousands are already **7.** _____

3 **Today**

- used for **8.** _____ and in magazines, books, and movies
- English as a **9.** _____
- helps people to **10.** _____ , share knowledge, and build up modern societies

WRITING AND DISCUSSION

Read the questions below and write down your ideas or opinions.
Exchange your ideas or opinions with your classmates. Use the hints
if you want.

1. Do you think English is needed in Japan? Why or why not?

    Hints ➡ to work and communicate / other languages

    Your Ideas

    ....
    ....
    ....
    ....
    ....

2. Do you think Japanese should be spread around the world? Why or why not?

    Hints ➡ to tell others about Japanese culture / difficult language / English is a common language

    Your Ideas

    ....
    ....
    ....
    ....
    ....

FURTHER STUDY

For further study, access ActeaBo and review today's lesson.

http://acteabo.jp

UNIT 1
UNIT 2
UNIT 3
UNIT 4
UNIT 5
UNIT 6
UNIT 7
UNIT 8
UNIT 9
UNIT 10
UNIT 11
UNIT 12
UNIT 13
UNIT 14
THE IMPORTANCE OF LANGUAGE

Tips for Reading: Reflecting on your study

Now that you have completed this textbook, how much have your English abilities improved? On Page 7, you set your goal and smaller steps. How many steps have you taken now?

Now is the time for you to stop and reflect on your learning.

- How much have you achieved?

- Was your method of learning OK?

- Is there anything you should change? If so, how?

LET'S TRY

Reflect on your English learning.

Your original goal	
Your original smaller steps	
How much you have achieved	
Things to change	

TEXT PRODUCTION STAFF

edited by	編集
Takashi Kudo	工藤 隆志

cover design by	表紙デザイン
Nobuyoshi Fujino	藤野 伸芳

text design by	本文デザイン
Nobuyoshi Fujino	藤野 伸芳

CD PRODUCTION STAFF

recorded by	吹き込み者
Jennifer Okano (AmE)	ジェニファー・オカノ（アメリカ英語）

Success with Reading Book 1 —Boost Your Reading Skills—
リーディング力アップのための7つの方略 Book 1

2020年1月20日　初版発行
2023年3月10日　第4刷発行

著 者	池田　真生子
	清水　綾香
	Michelle Witte
	Zachary Fillingham
	Gregory John Bahlmann
発 行 者	佐野 英一郎
発 行 所	株式会社 成美堂

〒101-0052　東京都千代田区神田小川町3-22
TEL 03-3291-2261　FAX 03-3293-5490
https://www.seibido.co.jp

印刷・製本　（株）加藤文明社

ISBN 978-4-7919-7201-2　　　　　　　　　　　Printed in Japan